Published in 2013
by Igloo Books Ltd
Cottage Farm
Sywell
NN6 0BJ
www.igloobooks.com

SHE001 0913
2 4 6 8 10 9 7 5 3 1
ISBN 978-1-78197-918-1

Printed and manufactured in China

FORMULA 1

The complete history of F1

Contents

Introduction

No sooner had the first motor cars been developed at the end of the 19th century than drivers started competing to see who could go further and faster. In 1894 the Paris to Rouen trial saw 21 cars competing for a 5,000 Franc first prize, which was awarded jointly to Panhard et Levassor and Peugeot for displaying the best combination of safety, economy, and ease of driving. It was a popular event and the following year, 1895, what is now held to be the world's first motor race was devised.

Formula One is still the world's greatest motorsport series. It's exciting, exhilarating, prestigious, and the only championship that is genuinely global in its reach.

LEFT: Sebastian Vettel (Toro Rosso STR03 Ferrari) in action during the 2008 Japanese Grand Prix at the Fuji Speedway.

Fernando Alonso drives during the third practice session at the Yas Marina circuit on November 3, 2012 in Abu Dhabi ahead of the Abu Dhabi Formula One Grand Prix.

Argentine Grand Prix

AUTÓDROME OSCAR JUAN Y GÁLVEZ

The Autódromo Oscar Juan y Gálvez in Buenos Aires has not been used for the Argentine Grand Prix since 1998, despite its fine facilities. Instead, it is now used both for national motor racing meetings and for hosting major outdoor events.

The track was first developed in 1952 by Argentine President Juan Péron, who wanted to attract the world's attention to the achievements of the country's best known and most successful racing driver, Juan Manuel Fangio. The circuit was duly constructed on what had been marshland just outside Buenos Aires.

When it was first opened, the circuit consisted of a newly built inner circuit combined with some existing local roads, creating a 3.6 mile (5.75 km) track with 15 turns. After being extended to include a lakeside section with two fast straights (Recto del Longo and Recto del Lago) it became the first truly international racing circuit in South America.

In the very last Formula One race held at the circuit, in 1998, David Coulthard took pole position though the race itself was won by Michael Schumacher. After that, financial problems made it impossible for further races to be held in Buenos Aires.

Below: Giuseppe Farina (Ferrari 625/555) leads Karl Kling (Mercedes-Benz W196) during the 1955 Argentine Grand Prix.

⬤ AUTÓDROMO OSCAR ALFREDO GÁLVEZ

TYPE:	purpose-built
LOCATION:	Buenos Aires
CIRCUIT LENGTH:	3.61 miles (5.81 km)
LAP RECORD:	1:27.981
	(G Berger/Benetton-Renault 1997)

Australian Grand Prix

ALBERT PARK

Following safety concerns after a high-speed accident in free practice in Adelaide in 1995, the Australian Grand Prix moved to Albert Park in Melbourne. At the time, officials in Australia were negotiating to bring the Pacific Grand Prix to the country, which, with their own Australian Grand Prix, would have given them two races.

Situated only around a mile from the skyscrapers of the Central Business District, the Melbourne Grand Prix's 3.29 mile (5.29 km) circuit backdrop consists of public roads. Despite its 16 corners, it is one of the fastest street circuits in the world, with top speeds of over 185 mph (300 kph), and average lap times of around 140 mph (225 kph). Because the track consists of conventional road tarmac, traction in the early stages of the Grand Prix weekend is always an issue until a "racing line" is laid down over the course of the race weekend. It's also a tough track for both drivers and machinery since as many as 3,500 gear-changes are made during the race and full-throttle is used for three-quarters of an average lap. Further difficulties are caused by the fact that the track is bumpy and has very limited run-off areas, so a sound chassis is essential for success and to avoid making high-speed contact with the walls.

Right: Lewis Hamilton, (McLaren MP4-23 Mercedes) leads during the 2008 Australian Grand Prix at Albert Park.

>>>>

● ALBERT PARK

TYPE:	city park
LOCATION:	Melbourne, Australia
CIRCUIT LENGTH:	3.29 miles (5.29 km)
LAP RECORD:	1:24.125
	(M Schumacher/Ferrari 2004)

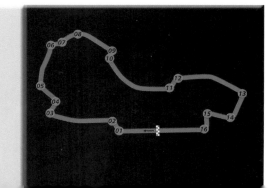

15

Kimi Räikkönen—who went on to win the race in his Ferrari F2007—leads the field on the opening lap of the 2007 Australian Grand Prix at Albert Park.

*A*ustrian Grand Prix

A1 RING

With the Alps creating a backbone for much of Austria, it comes as no surprise to discover that the A1-Ring, near Spielberg, is far from flat. In fact, it was developed using part of the winding and very fast Österreichring, which was renowned for its hilly terrain.

The A1-Ring is a very fast circuit with only ten corners during its 2.68 miles (4.31 km) lap. It also boasts four straights, and even though two of them have slight kinks, the circuit sees drivers revving right up to the red line and reaching speeds of up to 190 mph (304 kph) before going hard on the brakes for a succession of epic corners, including the Remus, Gösser, Niki Lauda, Jochen Rindt, and Castrol Kurves.

Formula One first came to the A1-Ring in 1997 after Hermann Tilke thoroughly revised the circuit, though concerns about safety resulted in it later losing its

place on the F1 calendar in 2003. The circuit itself is now owned by Dietrick Mateschitz, owner of the Red Bull energy drink and the Formula One teams named after it. However, attempts to bring Formula One back to the A1-Ring have failed despite repeated efforts by Mateschitz to attract top level racing back.

Below: Michael Schumacher (Ferrari F2003 GA) punches the air to celebrate his race win during the 2003 Austrian Grand Prix at A1-Ring.

A1 RING

TYPE:	purpose-built
LOCATION:	Spielberg, Austria
CIRCUIT LENGTH:	2.68 miles (4.31 km)
LAP RECORD:	1:08.337
	(M Schumacher/Ferrari 2003)

Bahrain Grand Prix

BAHRAIN INTERNATIONAL CIRCUIT

Right: Takuma Sato (BAR Honda 006) leads Jenson Button (BAR Honda 006) into turn one of the 2004 Bahrain Grand Prix. >>>>

The Bahrain International Circuit was the worthy recipient of the inaugural FIA Institute Center of Excellence Trophy in 2007. First opened in 2004 following an investment of some $150 million, it's a state-of-the-art motorsport circuit built in the desert around 20 miles (32 km) south of Bahrain's capital Manama.

The 3.36 miles (5.41 km) lap of the Grand Prix track consists of 15 corners and four straights, the longest of which is 1,192 yards (1,090 m) from start to finish. There's plenty of variation, as the track rises and falls nearly 20 yards (18 m) and varies in width from 15 to 24 yards (14 to 22 m). Created from scratch out in the desert, construction involved excavating 34 million square feet (968,459 cubic meters) of rock; laying 132,000 tonnes (120,000 metric tons) of asphalt and 18.5 million gallons (70,000 cubic meters) of concrete; erecting 13,000 yards (12,000 m) of guard rails and 5,500 yards (5,000 m) of

FIA safety fencing; placing 82,000 tires, and even laying 6,000 square yards (5,000 square meters) of grass carpet.

When it hosted the 2004 race, Bahrain was the very first Grand Prix to be held in the Middle East. The 2012 Grand Prix was one of the most controversial races in Formula One history when it went ahead despite political unrest, protests and human rights organizations calling for the race to be boycotted.

⬤ BAHRAIN INTERNATIONAL CIRCUIT

TYPE:	purpose-built
LOCATION:	Manama, Bahrain
CIRCUIT LENGTH:	3.36 miles (5.41 km)
LAP RECORD:	1:32.408
	(Nico Rosberg/
	Williams-Cosworth 2006)

0002234.567
450.45
9834568.234
44567.343
366585
557686.575

Lewis Hamilton (R) of Great Britain, McLaren and team mate Jenson Button (L) of Great Britain, McLaren drive side-by-side during the Brazilian Formula One Grand Prix at the Autódromo José Carlos Pace.

British Grand Prix

SILVERSTONE

There is a large sign outside the gates of Silverstone that proudly declares that this is "The Home of British Motorsport." When the Royal Automobile Club started looking for a venue where motor racing activities could be restarted, the disused airfields of Silverstone on the Northamptonshire/Buckinghamshire border looked ideal.

The original track was 3.67 miles (5.9 km) long. A chicane was added in 1975 to slow drivers before the notorious Woodcote Corner and changes were made at Bridge in 1987. In 1990/91, a major redesign resulted in the creation of the Luffield Complex and introduced some elevation to other parts of the track.

Despite the changes, Silverstone remains one of the fastest of all Grand Prix circuits, and during the Grand Prix weekend its main runway becomes Britain's busiest airport and heliport. From the start opposite the pits there's a fast right-hander at Copse which is followed by Maggotts, Becketts, and Chapel curves. Then it's into the extremely fast Hangar Straight, at the end of which is Stowe Corner, followed by the dip into Vale and a very challenging 90-degree left and the gradually unwinding right of Club Corner. After Abbey Curve, there's the short Farm Straight, then under Bridge for first Priory, followed by Luffield and finally Woodcote, and back on to the start/finish straight.

Right: Jean Alesi (Benetton B196 Renault) leads Mika Häkkinen (McLaren MP4/11 Mercedes) and Michael Schumacher (Ferrari F310) during the 1996 British Grand Prix at Silverstone. >>>>>>>>>

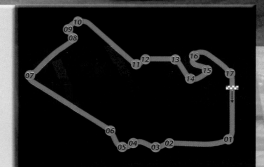

⦿ SILVERSTONE CIRCUIT

TYPE:	purpose-built airfield
LOCATION:	Silverstone, England
CIRCUIT LENGTH:	3.18 miles (5.12 km)
LAP RECORD:	1:18.739
	(M Schumacher/Ferrari 2004)

Virgin sponsored Brawn Formula One car at Silverstone circuit July 10, 2011, British Grand Prix.

British Grand Prix

BRANDS HATCH

Brands Hatch, in Kent, in the southeast of England is one of the truly great British motor racing venues. Its location, 20 miles (32 km) southeast of London, was a perfect spectator draw.

At the end of the start/finish straight is the blind Paddock Hill Bend right-hander which falls away sharply, before rising up Hailwood Hill to Druids Bend. Then it's downhill again to Graham Hill Bend, and along the short Cooper Straight behind the main paddock area, before the track goes sharply uphill and left at Surtees before the dip at Pilgrim's, Hawthorn Bend, and the Derek Minter Straight. The right-handed Westfield leads into yet another dip at Dingle Dell, followed by Sheene Curve and then Stirling's Bend, and on down to Clearways, Clark Curve, and finally back on to the Brabham Straight for the finish.

Between 1964 and 1986, the circuit hosted 12 British Grand Prix as well as the European Grand Prix in 1983 and 1985. Though no Grand Prixs have been held at Brands Hatch since, it remains the home of numerous top class racing events.

>>>>

Right: Riccardo Patrese (Brabham BT52B BMW) leads the field through Paddock Hill Bend at the start of the 1983 British and European Grand Prix at Brands Hatch.

🔘 BRANDS HATCH

TYPE:	purpose-built parkland
LOCATION:	Brands Hatch, England
CIRCUIT LENGTH:	2.60 miles (4.18 km)
LAP RECORD:	1:09.593
	(N Mansell/Williams-Honda 1986)

0002234.56
450.4
99834568.23
44567.343
366585

Druids Hill Bend, Brands Hatch at the start of the FIA Masters Historic Formula One Championship race May 27, 2013.

Caesar's Palace

CAESAR'S PALACE

<<< **Left:** Alan Jones (Williams FW07C Ford) leads going into Turn 1 on the first lap of the 1981 Caesar's Palace Grand Prix.

Money and Formula One go together like the proverbial horse and carriage, which was why the Grand Prix circus headed to Las Vegas after the contract to run the United States Grand Prix at Watkins Glen had expired.

From scratch, a 2.26 mile (3.64 km) circuit running in a counter-clockwise direction was built in Ceasar's Palace car park and yet there was so much space available that most drivers said that despite the debilitating effect of the desert sun, they enjoyed the venue because it left them plenty of space for overtaking. For safety's sake, generous sand-filled run-off areas were provided to slow down cars unfortunate enough to slide off the mirror-like road surface. In fact, there was so little grip that watching the drivers battle with their sliding cars added considerably to the thrill of the event. And since spectators could get very close to the action, it was an unrivaled opportunity to catch the excitement of Grand Prix racing at close quarters.

Only two Formula One Championship races were held at Las Vegas, in 1981 and 1982, though two further non-championship events were held in 1983 and 1984. After that, Las Vegas returned to its roots as America's leading vacation and gambling resort.

CAESAR'S PALACE

TYPE:	city center car park
LOCATION:	Las Vegas, United States
CIRCUIT LENGTH:	2.26 miles (3.64 km)
LAP RECORD:	1:19.639
	(M Alboreto/Tyrrell-Cosworth1982)

Canadian Grand Prix

CIRCUIT GILLES VILLENEUVE

Circuit Gilles Villeneuve is named after the French-Canadian superstar who was tragically killed in an accident while qualifying his Ferrari at the Zolder Circuit in Belgium. It is held on a man-made island in the St Lawrence River, on the site originally constructed for the 1976 Montreal Olympics.

The Canadian Grand Prix has been held in the city of Montreal since 1978; despite the fact that the circuit was purpose-designed, in many ways it has the atmosphere of a street circuit, partly because of its limited run-off areas and partly due to the majestic backdrop of the skyscrapers of downtown Montreal. Circuit Gilles Villeneuve is faster than any street circuit and its 2.71 mile (4.36 km) lap is a constant challenge to the teams and their drivers.

There are 15 corners in total, of which six are chicane-type complexes. There is also a long and very fast straight running from the Virage Du Casino to the start/finish area, which provides one of the most enthralling hard braking and tight turn-in sections, at its pit-lane entrance end. Here, drivers "kiss the wall" at the exit, getting as close as possible to the unyielding concrete that bears the legend "Bienvenue au Quebec."

Below: Jean Alesi (Ferrari 412T2) on the way to his maiden Grand Prix win at the 1995 Canadian Grand Prix at the Circuit Gilles Villenueve.

∨∨∨∨

CIRCUIT GILLES VILLENEUVE

TYPE:	purpose-built city
LOCATION:	Montreal, Canada
CIRCUIT LENGTH:	2.71 miles (4.36 km)
LAP RECORD:	1:13.622 (R Barrichello/Ferrari 2004)

Mark Webber, Red Bull Racing at the Formula 1 Canadian Grand
Prix in Montreal, Canada on Saturday, June 9, 2012.

Chinese Grand Prix

SHANGHAI INTERNATIONAL CIRCUIT

Claimed to be the most advanced Grand Prix track in the world, the Shanghai International Circuit was built from scratch on reclaimed swampland and completed in May 2004 at a cost of some $450 million.

The circuit itself can accommodate up to 200,000 people and is characterized by its distinctive main buildings, which bridge the track at either end of the start/finish area and give diners in the splendid Sky Restaurant a unique view of the racing below.

The challenging 3.37 mile (5.42 km) circuit has 16 turns, interspersed by two long straights. The first three turns occur in quick succession after the start/finish area, followed by a fourth that opens out into a faster stretch punctuated by the gentle kink of Turn 5. After the extended hairpin of Turn 6, the track opens out again briefly for the gentler Turns 7 and 8. Then it closes up again for Turns 9 and 10, before the short straight that precedes the slower, more difficult Turns 11, 12, and 13. This complex is followed by one of the longest straights in Formula One, culminating in the tortuous right hairpin of Turn 14, another kink right and then the 90-degree left-hand turn into the start/finish area. The Shanghai International Circuit has quickly become a favorite with drivers and spectators.

>>>

Right: Lewis Hamilton (McLaren MP4-23 Mercedes)—finished first—leads Kimi Räikkönen (Ferrari F2008)—finished third—and Felipe Massa (Ferrari F2008)—finished second—during the 2008 Chinese Grand Prix.

⬤ SHANGHAI INTERNATIONAL CIRCUIT

TYPE:	purpose-built
LOCATION:	Shanghai, China
CIRCUIT LENGTH:	3.37 miles (5.42 km)
LAP RECORD:	1:32.238
	(M Schumacher/Ferrari 2004)

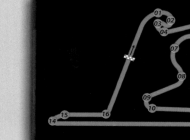

0002234.5
450.
99834568.2
44567.34
36658
35657686.57

Italian Grand Prix

AUTODROMO NAZIONALE MONZA

The Autodromo Nazionale di Monza, located within a park to the north of the city of the same name, is the most famous motor racing circuit in Italy and one of the best-known in the world.

Monza's circuit was always a high-speed layout that incorporated both a 3.4 mile (5.5 km) road track and a 2.8 mile (4.5 km) oval with banked sections that boosted top speeds without unduly compromising safety. The original Grand Prix road track has remained largely unaltered for most of its existence.

In common with other famous motor racing venues, Monza's corners have become famous throughout the world. They include the Variante del Rettifilo, the tight chicane that's the first hazard the drivers meet after the start of the race. This is followed by the fast Curva Grande and yet another chicane at Variante della Roggia. A short straight is then followed by the challenging double right-handed Curve di Lesmo, which in turn leads onto the equally challenging Curva del Serraglio. From here, there's a short straight under the original banked oval and into the fast Variante Ascari chicane. This is followed by another short straight and finally into the long right-handed 180-degree Curva Parabolica that leads back to the start/finish straight.

Right: Michael Schumacher >>>> (Ferrari 248F1) in the lead during the 2006 Italian Grand Prix at Monza.

AUTODROMO NAZIONALE MONZA

TYPE:	permanent circuit
LOCATION:	9.3 miles (15 km) northeast of Milan, Italy
CIRCUIT LENGTH:	3.59 miles (5.78 km)
LAP RECORD:	1:21.046 (R Barrichello/Ferrari 2004)

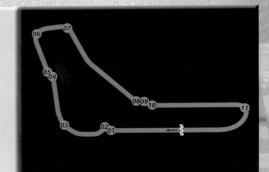

Fernando Alonso in a Ferrari F10 races in the Italian
Grand Prix, on September 11, 2010 in Monza, Italy.

Japanese Grand Prix

SUZUKA CIRCUIT

Suzuka International Racing Course is one of the few circuits in the world to employ a figure-of-eight crossover layout. At a total length of 3.6 miles (5.80 km), its intricate and highly technical layout offers a considerable challenge for drivers: in particular, the changes in elevation create a number of blind bends where judging the exit can be difficult.

Below: Fernando Alonso (Renault R26) passes Ralf Schumacher (Toyota TF106B) on his way to winning the 2006 Japanese Grand Prix at Suzuka.

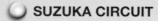

⚪ SUZUKA CIRCUIT

TYPE:	permanent circuit
LOCATION:	Suzuka City, Japan
CIRCUIT LENGTH:	3.6 miles (5.80 km)
LAP RECORD:	1:31.540
	(K Räikkönen/McLaren 2005)

A lap of the track commences one-third of the way up the start/finish straight, which leads into the extended right-handed hairpin of Turn 1—also known as First. After a short straight comes a sequence of five bends, culminating in the fast Dunlop left-hander which leads into the mid-speed right at Degner and a tighter right at Turn 9. The circuit then ducks under the crossover bridge to the fast right-hander at Turn 10, followed by the sharply left-handed Hairpin. Drivers continue through another double-apex right-hander and on to the very fast Spoon—an extended left-hander that leads to the Crossover, the fastest stretch of the track. This is followed by the incredibly challenging left-handed 130R, which has undergone extensive modification following serious accidents in 2002 and 2003. Finally, it's into the Casio Triangle, three corners numbered 15, 16, and 17, which effectively meld into one long right hander that opens onto the start of the finishing straight.

0002234.56
450.4
99834568.23
44567.343
366585
35657686.57

Adrian Sutil of Force India-Mercedes during free practice at 2011 Formula 1 Japanese Grand Prix on October 7, 2011 in Suzuka, Japan.

Korean Grand Prix

KOREA INTERNATIONAL CIRCUIT

Despite military tensions within Korea, in 2010 Formula One debuted at the Korea International Circuit in South Korea. It was welcomed into the Formula One family after a deal between Bernie Ecclestone and Korean Formula One promoter Auto Valley Operation.

One of the most recognized and respected track designers, Hermann Tilke from Germany, was engaged in 2009 to design the track. He created a part-permanent and part-temporary track along the harbor front, with some of the city streets being used for the pit lane. Finishing the construction on time proved to be a very close-run thing, with Korea missing the FIA technical inspection scheduled for 28th September 2010, despite announcing at the end of 2009 that everything was on track. This inspection is crucial, as a Formula One license can only be awarded once the inspection is passed. In the event, the two-day inspection took place 11 days before the first practice sessions were due to start and the license was issued through the Korea Automobile Racing Association.

The circuit starts with a double left hander; the first corner is taken in second gear, with the drivers accelerating through the second turn. This opens up onto a 0.75 miles (1.2 km) straight – the longest on a circuit in Asia – which in turn feeds into the slowest corner on the circuit, a second-gear right-hand bend. The cars follow a shorter straight, home to the support pits, before a series of tight switchbacks at Turns 4, 5 and 6; all three are taken in second gear. The circuit then opens up again, flowing through a series of fast fifth-gear bends, before the driver must brake for Turn 10, a tight right-hander whose approach is made more difficult by the position of the braking zone on a downward-sloping incline. The remainder of the circuit is modeled on a street circuit, and follows a labyrinth series of left and right-hand bends that lead to Turn 17, a long right-hander that is completely blind as it is surrounded by walls. The final turn on the circuit is a left-hand kink that feeds onto the main straight.

Below: Atmosphere during the Korean Formula One Grand Prix at the Korea International Circuit on October 14, 2012.

⊙ KOREA INTERNATIONAL CIRCUIT

TYPE:	part temporary, part permanent circuit
LOCATION:	Yeongham, 250 miles (400 km) south of Seoul
CIRCUIT LENGTH:	3.49 miles (5.62 km)
LAP RECORD:	1:39.605 (Sebastian Vettel/Red Bull 2011)

The pit lane has been one of the most contested features of the Korea International Circuit. In 2010, drivers criticized placing the entry on the racing line exit of a corner that is taken at speeds in excess of 150 mph. This meant that those pitting would be driving dangerously slow on the racing line. The pit lane exit has also been criticized as it feeds into the outside of Turn 1. In 2011, Nico Rosberg, Mercedes, locked up at the turn and ran wide, colliding with Jaime Alguersuari, Toro Rosso, although that particular incident didn't actually occur on the racing line.

Top: Start of the Korean Formula One Grand Prix at the Korea International Circuit.

0002234.567
450.45
99834568.234
44567.3435
3665854
35657686.575

Sebastian Vettel of Germany, Red Bull Racing drives in for a pit stop on his way to finishing second during the Korean Formula One Grand Prix at the Korea International Circuit on October 14, 2012.

Malaysian Grand Prix

SEPANG INTERNATIONAL CIRCUIT

Built on the site of a former palm oil plantation, the Sepang International Circuit was completed in a record 14 months and was opened on March 9, 1999, by the Prime Minister of Malaysia.

Sepang's astonishing facilities include an enormous three-storey Pit Building which, as well as the 33 pits, contains all the management offices and officials' quarters. Next door is the Welcome Building which boasts shops, restaurants, and an exhibition center. On the other side of the Pit Building is a Medical Center that can be converted in an emergency into a fully-equipped hospital, complete with operating theaters.

The centrally located main grandstands guarantee fantastic views of the action, and can seat 32,000 people as well as accommodating various corporate entertainment suites.

At just under 3.5 miles (5.54 km) long, the full Sepang Grand Prix circuit contains 15 turns and eight straights, which means some of the highest top speeds in Formula One are seen here. The width of the track also offers plenty of overtaking opportunities. The unique parallel configuration of the start/finish and back straights, with just a single hairpin in between them, allows the track to be divided into North and South circuits for smaller events, such as kart racing.

>>>>

Right: Felipe Massa (Ferrari F2008) leads the field at the start of the 2008 Malaysian Grand Prix.

SEPANG INTERNATIONAL CIRCUIT

TYPE:	permanent circuit
LOCATION:	Kuala Lumpur, Malaysia
CIRCUIT LENGTH:	3.44 miles (5.54 km)
LAP RECORD:	1:34.223 (J P Montoya/Williams-BMW 2004)

0101010101010101010101010101010101010101010101010101010101010
0101010101010101010101010101010101010101010101010101010101010
0101010101010101010101010101010101010101010101010101010101010
0101010101010101010101010101010101010101010101010101010101010   0002234.56
0101010101010101010101010101010101010101010101010101010101010   450.4
0101010101010101010101010101010101010101010101010101010101010   99834568.23
                                                                   44567.343
                                                                     366585
                                                                  35657686.57

Nico Rosberg of Germany, Mercedes Team at top speed on the main straight at the Malaysian Formula 1 Grand Prix April 4, 2010.

Moroccan Grand Prix

AIN-DIAB

Moroccan interest in motor racing dates back to 1925, when a Grand Prix was held in the Atlantic coastal city of Casablanca during the days when the nation was still a French dependency.

Formula One motor racing returned to Morocco in 1954 at a sports car circuit in the southern coastal resort of Agadir, where it remained for two years. But in 1957 came the Suez Crisis, which threatened to play havoc with the Grand Prix calendar due to the fuel shortages and transportation difficulties which resulted from the closure of the Suez Canal. Seizing what he perceived as a golden opportunity to supplant one of the big European Grand Prix, Sultan Mohammed V ordered the hasty construction of the Ain-Diab Street Circuit in Casablanca—a project that was completed in just six weeks.

The following year, an officially sanctioned Grand Prix did take place on the dusty Ain-Diab track and was won by Englishman Stirling Moss driving a Vanwall. Sadly, the event was marred by the horrific crash of Moss's team-mate Stuart Lewis-Evans, whose engine seized (reputedly due to the dust) and sent him plunging into the barriers, his car in flames. His death cast a shadow over the Grand Prix, which saw the Formula One circus abandon Morocco, never to return.

Above: Stirling Moss (Vanwall VW5) during his winning drive at the 1958 Moroccan Grand Prix.

● AIN-DIAB

TYPE:	street circuit
LOCATION:	Ain-Diab, Morocco
CIRCUIT LENGTH:	4.75 miles (7.64 km)
LAP RECORD:	2:22.500 (S Moss/Vanwall 1958)

Portuguese Grand Prix

AUTÓDROMO DO ESTORIL

Built in Estoril, the seaside resort near Lisbon, the new Autódromo do Estoril soon became a favorite with drivers thanks to its elevation changes and its tight and difficult nature.

After hosting many junior formulae and Formula Two European Championship races during the 1970s, a total of 13 Grand Prix were held there between 1984 and 1996. Following the deaths of Ayrton Senna and Austrian driver Roland Ratzenburger at Imola in 1994, the circuit's organizers became increasingly preoccupied with safety. The 2.72 mile (4.38 km) layout was modified to replace the very fast Tanque Corner with a much slower complex of corners known collectively as Gancho, and the Parabolica bend leading on to the start/finish straight was renamed in Senna's honor.

Although Grand Prix racing continued at Estoril for another three seasons, it became clear that even in its modified form, the circuit was simply too dangerous for the latest generation of Formula One cars. It did continue hosting major events including the FAI GT Championships, the DTM series, and more recently a round of the A1 Grand Prix and even the Portuguese Motorcycle Grand Prix. Estoril was suggested as the venue for the 1997 European Grand Prix, but in the end it was decided it could not reach the required safety standards so the idea was dropped.

Below: Rubens Barrichello (Jordan 195 Peugeot) leads Mika Häkkinen and Mark Blundell (both McLaren MP4/10B Mercedes) during the 1995 Portuguese Grand Prix at Estoril.

● AUTÓDROMO DO ESTORIL

TYPE:	permanent circuit
LOCATION:	Estoril, Portugal
CIRCUIT LENGTH:	2.72 miles (4.38 km)
LAP RECORD:	1:22.446
	(D Coulthard/Williams-Renault 1994)

0002234.56
450.4
99834568.23
44567.343
366585

San Marino Grand Prix

AUTODROMO ENZO E DINO FERRARI

The Imola circuit, in the foothills of the Apennine Mountains, was opened in 1952, although the nearby parkland had been used for motocross races for some years before. But it would not be until 1963 that the first Grand Prix was held at the circuit, a non-Championship event that was won by Scots driver Jim Clark in a Lotus-Climax.

The track was at first named for the Santerno River which runs alongside it, but Imola was officially renamed the Autodromo Enzo e Dino Ferrari after the death of Enzo Ferrari and his son Dino.

The circuit has been changed many times over the years, most notably by the addition of three chicanes—the Variante Bassa in 1973, the Variante Alta in 1974, and the Acque Minerale in 1981—to slow cars down. There have also been alterations to the very fast Tamburello corner, the scene of many terrifying accidents over the years, not least the one in 1994 that killed Ayrton Senna. Villeneuve Corner, where Roland Ratzenberger was killed, was also modified after that year's tragic events. The last Formula One race was held at Imola in 2006, and while motor racing continues at the venue, it remains to be seen if Formula One will ever return.

Above:
Fernando Alonso (Renault R26) during a pitstop at the 2006 San Marino Grand Prix.

<< **Left:**
Michael Schumacher (Ferrari 248F1) leads Jenson Button (HondaRA106) early in the 2006 San Marino Grand Prix. Schumacher went on to win the race.

⬤ AUTODROMO ENZO E DINO FERRARI

TYPE:	permanent circuit
LOCATION:	Imola, 25 miles (40 km) east of Bologna, Italy
CIRCUIT LENGTH:	3.06 miles (4.93 km)
LAP RECORD:	1:20.411 (M Schumacher/Ferrari 2004)

Lewis Hamilton, Sebastian Vettel and Fernando Alonso celebrate in November 2012 after the United States Grand Prix was held in Travis County, Texas.

The 1950s

Formula One began in 1950, two years after the inauguration of a new governing body for motorsport, the FIA. Plans for two championships—constructors and drivers—were unveiled in a bid to provide some structure to the races going on around the world.

The championship united six main European races—Britain, Monaco, Switzerland, Belgium, France, and Italy—with the Indianapolis 500 in the United States.

<<<< **Left:** Jack Brabham (Cooper T51-Climax) leads Tony Brooks (Ferrari Dino 246) and Harry Schell (BRM P25) during the 1959 Dutch Grand Prix.

1950

The first-ever race of the new Formula One world championship took place at the converted airfield of Silverstone, in the heart of Great Britain, and right from the start it was clear that Italian racing red was the order of the day.

Ferrari failed to make it to the opening race at Silverstone, and Alfa filled the first three places on the grid then went on to fill all three places on the podium in Monaco for the second race.

The Indianapolis race was only part of the championship because of its status as one of the world's great races, but none of the European teams turned up and American Johnny Parsons took a victory for Wynn's Kurtis that secured him sixth in the championship. Back in Europe, Alfa men Fangio and Farina traded victories well ahead of the chasing pack and in a dramatic final race at Monza, a gearbox failure for Fangio gave Farina the win and the title by three points.

Below: Alberto Ascari (Ferrari 125, number 40) passes the multi-car accident at the start of the 1950 Monaco Grand Prix.

1951

Ferrari were driving forward, but Alfa still set the early pace in 1951, with Fangio winning in rainy Switzerland.

The first victory for Ferrari finally came at Silverstone when Froilán González capitalized on a mistake by fellow Argentine Fangio. Later, Ascari claimed his first win, because the long straights of the Nürburgring, a new addition to the calendar, suited his Ferrari.

The final race was on the Pedrables street circuit in Spain, which was also destined to be the last race for Alfa before they quit the sport. Thanks to the talent of Fangio and tire problems that beset his title rival Ascari's Ferrari, it was a happy ending for Alfa. The Argentine won, and took the title.

1952

With Alfa gone, Ferrari were now the dominant force in Formula One. The open rules allowed many new teams to join Italians Ferrari and Maserati, with the British Cooper-Bristol in the hands of Mike Hawthorn, and French Gordini machines the best of the rest. But they would never be close enough to challenge the establishment.

Having failed to win at Indianapoils, with victory there going to Troy Ruttman in his Kurtis-Kraft, Ascari returned for round three, in Belgium, and dominated the rest of the season with an amazing run of six consecutive race victories, with the fastest lap in every one.

He mastered the wet in Spa then led a Ferrari 1-2-3 in France and a 1-2 in Britain. Victories in Holland and Italy finished off a remarkable run of dominance and, with only the best four results counting, Ascari notched up a perfect score.

1958

It was the end of an era when Fangio and Maserati retired from Formula One in 1958.

In the longest Formula One season so far, Vanwall seemed to be Ferrari's only rivals, but it was a rear-engined Cooper-Climax 43 (as opposed to the then-standard front-engined design) that claimed the first victory with Moss at the wheel.

It was not going to plan for Ferrari and, though they won in France, with Hawthorn taking his only victory of the year, tragedy struck as Musso was killed. Briton Collins won for Ferrari at Silverstone but, just two weeks later, he was also killed, becoming the second Ferrari driver to lose his life in a month.

1959

The end of the decade marked a true phase shift in Formula One as the rear-engined Cooper-Climax, with a new 2.5-liter engine, came to the fore.

Vanwall had quit and Brooks had joined Ferrari, along with Behra and American Phil Hill, but their front-engined machine failed to perform and a new grid order was created.

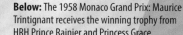
Below: The 1958 Monaco Grand Prix: Maurice Trintignant receives the winning trophy from HRH Prince Rainier and Princess Grace.

The 1960s

This 10-year period saw Formula One go through what could be seen as the most significant technical developments in its history. British teams led the way and the sport began to build its reputation as the place for innovation at the pinnacle of motorsport.

The arrival of sponsorship put an end to teams racing in national colors and, as the sport headed into the 1970s, the 13-race calendar could now claim to be fully global, with a core in Europe, but races also run in South Africa, Canada, the United States, and Mexico.

<<<< **Left:** The cars line up on the grid before the start of the 1966 British Grand Prix.

1960

The success of Jack Brabham and his Cooper at the end of the 1950s left nobody in any doubt that the front-engined car had had its day. Nevertheless, Ferrari persisted and got nowhere. Instead, Cooper and the new rear-engined Lotus dominated, with Brabham and Bruce McLaren taking on Moss and Innes Ireland.

Below: Jack Brabham (Cooper T53 Climax) on his way to victory in the 1960 Monaco Grand Prix.

The European field now included Belgium, but it was one of the worst races in history. Moss had a leg-breaking crash; then, as Brabham raced from pole to victory, Chris Bristow and Alan Stacey were killed, the latter after his helmet was hit by a bird.

Brabham claimed further victories in France, Britain, and Portugal, where he won the title with two races to go. With the championship over, the British teams boycotted the Italian race due to safety concerns, so Phil Hill won for Ferrari while Moss returned to finish off the season with victory at the final round in the United States.

1966

Stewart won the opening race in Monaco for BRM, but the second race was at a rain-hit Spa circuit in Belgium and the Scot had a terrible crash that sidelined him for two months. Surtees won in what would be his last race for Ferrari before his switch to Cooper.

All the title contenders, including Brabham, retired from the race at Monza, handing Surtees his third world title as rookie Ludovico Scarfiotti won for Ferrari.

1967

The arrival of the new Lotus 49 coupled with a revolutionary Cosworth DFV engine tempted Hill to join rival Clark in what many saw as the dream team for 1967.

Hulme took early victories for Brabham and the championship moved on to Holland, where the Lotus 49 made its debut and Clark drove to victory.

Reliability problems marred the Lotus season. Clark ran out of fuel while leading at Monza, handing victory to Surtees and Honda, then the Lotus finally found some reliability, which allowed Clark to lead a 1-2. But it was too little, too late, and Hulme claimed the crown.

Below: Jackie Stewart (BRM P83) before the start of the 1967 British Grand Prix.

1968

Hill, now racing in a newly sponsored red, white, and gold Lotus fitted with aerodynamic wings, scored victories in Spain and Monaco. Racing continued, and after Jo Siffert won in Britain in a private Lotus, Stewart took victory at Germany's Nürburgring and Hulme won in Monza and Canada, moving him level with Hill in the championship.

Victory in the United States for Stewart set up a three-way season-ending title battle in Mexico. Hulme crashed out early, but Stewart and Hill vied for the lead until the Scot suffered handling problems and dropped down the order, leaving Hill to win the title.

1969

Stewart dominated the season opener in South Africa, then won again in Spain after Ferrari suffered engine problems and the two Lotus cars crashed heavily after failures to their high-mounted wings, which were subsequently banned from the sport.

Hill claimed his fifth win in Monaco, but it was just a minor break in Stewart's rhythm, and the Scot raced to further victories in Holland, France, and Britain. Ickx won in Canada after knocking Stewart out of the race and Rindt won in the United States, in a race marred by a major accident that saw Hill break both legs. He missed the season finale in Mexico, which was won by Hulme for McLaren.

Above: British driver Graham Hill, then reigning world champion, delighted after winning the Monaco Grand Prix. Graham Hill was Formula One world champion twice in 1962 and 1968.

Graham Hill leads Jo Siffert (both Lotus 49B Ford) and Jackie Stewart (Matra MS10 Ford) during the 1968 Mexican Grand Prix. They finished in first, sixth, and seventh positions respectively.

1971

Tyrrell decided to go it alone after a promising test for his own car at the end of the previous season and it proved to be a wise decision, as Stewart dominated and the rest of the field failed to produce a consistently strong contender.

Stewart won in France, Britain, and Germany, twice leading team-mate François Cevert home in a 1-2 for Tyrrell. BRM managed to stop his run of success when Jo Siffert won in Austria, but when Ickx retired from the race, the championship went to Stewart.

Peter Gethin snatched victory from Peterson by 0.01s in Italy as the top five cars crossed the line within 0.61s of each other. Stewart retired with engine failure in Monza, but won in Canada while his team-mate Cevery claimed his first win at the season finale in the United States.

1972

Bernie Ecclestone became team manager of Brabham and when Formula One returned to Argentina for race one, his home driver Carlos Reutermann took pole, though reigning champion Stewart raced past to win for Tyrrell.

However, Fittipaldi would soon stamp his authority with victory in four of the following six races. The Brazilian won in Belgium, with Stewart sidelined by a stomach ulcer, the consistent Fittipaldi extended his title lead over Stewart by winning in Austria then sealed the crown with victory in Monza.

1973

Lotus hoped to dominate when Peterson joined Fittipaldi in the 'dream team' and, though McLaren, Brabham, and March were all in the mix, it was the resurgent Stewart, in his Tyrrell, who led the fight to stop them.

Lotus returned to form in Austria, where Peterson waved Fittipaldi through for the sake of the title only for the Brazilian to retire. The pair finished 1-2 in Italy, but the title battle was over. The season wasn't, and after Revson won in the Canadian race Cevert was killed in practice in the United States. Peterson won, but the death of Stewart's team-mate vindicated the Scot's decision to quit.

Above: François Cevert (Tyrrell 006 Ford Cosworth) in action during the 1973 British Grand Prix.

1974

Fittipaldi moved from Lotus to McLaren when the team lured the major Marlboro sponsorship funding away from BRM. There was change at Ferrari, too, with a brand new car and the arrival of Regazzoni and Niki Lauda.

Peterson and Scheckter took second victories in France and Britain respectively, before Regazzoni finally won for Ferrari in Germany.

Reutermann won in Austria and Peterson in Italy but, after finishing first and second in Canada, Regazzoni and Fittipaldi fought for the title in the United States finale. They were level on points, but a disappointing finish saw Regazzoni drop down the field with handling problems, leaving Fittipaldi finishing fourth to claim the title.

Below: Emerson Fittipaldi crosses the finish line ahead of Niki Lauda, to take the win at the 1974 Belgian Grand Prix.

1975

After several years of British success, Ferrari introduced the new longitudinal gearboxed 312T and was ready to return to form. Lauda grew into a fine team leader, but a season to savour for the Italian giants was hit by more fatalities, making it a sad year for everyone involved in Formula One.

1976

Ferrari's champion Lauda faced a tough challenge from James Hunt in 1976 after the Briton replaced Fittipaldi at McLaren. In a nail-biting battle, Lauda suffered a serious accident but came back to take the championship right down to the wire.

Hunt started strongly, putting his McLaren on pole in Argentina and South Africa, but both times he lost out to Lauda in the race, then Regazzoni made it three for Ferrari with victory at a new Long Beach street race in the United States.

Lauda was well on course for the title when he crashed in Germany and suffered severe burns. Hunt moved to within three points of the lead, winning in Canada and the United States then, when Lauda pulled out of the last race in Japan on safety grounds after a torrential downpour, Hunt raced on and claimed the third place he needed to take the title.

>>>>

Right: James Hunt (McLaren M23 Ford) leads John Watson (Penske PC4 Ford) on his way to victory in the 1976 Dutch Grand Prix.

1977

Ferrari and Lauda put together a consistent campaign in a season that saw eight different winners from the 17 races. However, the year was again tainted by driver and spectator deaths.

A horrific accident in South Africa killed Tom Pryce and a track marshal. Then, sadly, Pace died in a plane crash before the next race.

Lauda won for Ferrari in Germany and Holland and took second places in Austria, where Alan Jones gave Shadow a first win, and Italy, where Andretti finished first for Lotus. Lauda had been third or better in all but one of the races he had finished and he secured the title with fourth place in the United States, a race won by Hunt.

1978

Ferrari introduced the new 312T3 in a bid to retain their superiority, but Lotus took another step forward with the revolutionary 79 and soon began to dominate the season. Their success, however, was soured by the tragic death of Ronnie Peterson.

A double Lotus retirement let Reutermann win for Ferrari in Britain, but Lotus then won in Germany, Austria, and Holland; the latter being their fourth 1-2 of the year as Peterson was forced to play second fiddle to Andretti. Only Peterson could beat Andretti to the title, but a fiery start-line crash in Italy saw him suffer terrible burns and, despite being quickly dragged from the wreckage by Hunt, Regazzoni, and Depallier, he died the following day.

Andretti was crowned Champion, but it was the Ferraris of Reutermann and Villeneuve that went on to win the last two races, in the US and Canada.

1979

The season started with victories for Laffitte's Ligier in Argentina and Brazil, but Ferrari introduced their new car for race three and Villeneuve led 1-2 finishes in South Africa and the United States. Ligier won again with Depallier in Spain, but Scheckter got his first Ferrari win in Belgium and followed it up with victory in Monaco.

Formula One history was made at Dijon in France, when the usually unreliable Renault made it across the finish line to claim the first-ever turbo-powered victory, with Jean-Pierre Jabouille leading home Arnoux after a dramatic wheel-to-wheel battle.

The new Williams FW07 had been competitive ever since its Belgian debut and in Britain, Jones put it on pole before Regazzoni secured the team their first-ever victory.

Scheckter took what would be Ferrari's last title for 21 years when he won in Italy, finishing just 0.46s ahead of Villeneuve in a Ferrari 1-2 as team tactics came into play.

<<<<

Left: Niki Lauda (Ferrari 312T2) battles with Mario Andretti (Lotus 78 Ford) on his way to winning the 1977 Dutch Grand Prix.

James Hunt (McLaren M23 Ford) locks up and takes off over the front wheel of John Watson's Brabham BT45B Alfa Romeo, in the chain reaction of collisions at Cooks Corner on the first lap of the 1977 United States Grand Prix.

The 1980s

The start of the decade was overshadowed by political rows as the manufacturer teams and the privateers vied for supremacy. The manufacturers, led by Ferrari, Renault and Alfa Romeo, were pushing for a limitation in the use of ground-effect aerodynamics, to help make the most of their turbo engines; while the smaller teams wanted no restrictions because they could not afford the cost of developing the new high-power engines.

Tragic accidents in the early 80s cut short the career of Didier Pironi and cost Gilles Villeneuve his life, leaving Brazilians Ayrton Senna and Nelson Piquet, Frenchman Alain Prost, and Briton Nigel Mansell as the men to watch.

Left: Gerhard Berger (Ferrari F187/88C) holds off Alain Prost (McLaren MP4/4 Honda) as they race through Casino Square during the 1988 Monaco Grand Prix. Prost went on to win the race.

1980

Williams built on the form they showed at the end of the 1970s while champions Ferrari lost their way and even failed to qualify for one race. Alfa Romeo returned and Brabham stepped up to the front. Safety continued to be an issue with several top drivers killed, paralysed, or lucky to escape.

Regazzoni's career was ended at the next race in the United States when he crashed and was left paralysed. Piquet scored his first victory in that race, for Brabham, then Pironi took his maiden win, for Ligier, in Belgium. Williams then began a run of victories when Reutermann took the spoils in Monaco and though Jones' victory in Spain was declared void after the turbo teams refused to take part, he went on to win in France and Britain.

Depallier died in a testing crash before the German race, which was won by Laffite, then Jean-Pierre Jabouille won for Renault in Austria.

The championship was decided in the next three races, with Piquet taking the lead by a point after wins in Holland and Italy and setting up a dramatic race in Canada. Jones and Piquet collided on the first lap, causing a race stoppage, but Piquet retired from the restart and Jones won the race then finished off in style with victory in the United States.

Below: Alan Jones (Williams FW07B-Ford Cosworth) in the 1980 British Grand Prix.

1988

McLaren took Honda from Williams for 1988 and Senna joined Prost in a new super team that completely crushed the opposition, winning 15 of the 16 races as Williams descended from dominant champions to mid-grid mediocrity.

Heavy rain at Silverstone saw Prost stop on safety grounds as Senna won ahead of Mansell in a shock second. Senna then took a hat-trick of wins in Germany, Hungary, and Belgium before his domination was stopped by a back marker in Italy and Ferrari scored a poignant 1-2 just weeks after Enzo Ferrari passed away.

Prost then looked set for victory in Japan when Senna dropped to 14th at the start but Senna raced back and overtook Prost to win. Senna—with 90 points and eight wins— had done enough to win his first title.

Below: Alain Prost (McLaren MP4/4 Honda) celebrates his victory in the 1988 Australian Grand Prix at Adelaide.

1989

A move to the new 3.5-liter non-turbo formula failed to stop another season of McLaren domination, but the rivalry between Senna and Prost boiled over as they tried to out-do each other in every way possible.

Mansell joined Ferrari with instant success, but the Italian team was not strong enough to mount a title challenge. Senna went on to dominant wins in Monaco and Mexico, but it was not to last and he suffered four retirements as Prost won in the United States, Boutsen broke McLaren's domination with a Williams 1-2 in Canada, and Prost won again in France and Britain.

Berger won in Portugal after Mansell took out Senna, leaving Prost with a 24-point lead. Senna would not give up and won in Spain then battled Prost for victory in Japan. The pair collided, putting Prost out, but Senna came back to win only to be disqualified, handing victory to Nannini's Benetton and the title to Prost.

Below: Ayrton Senna leads into the first corner followed by team-mate Alain Prost (both McLaren MP4/5 Honda) during the 1989 Belgian Grand Prix. Senna finished in first place and Prost in second.

The 1990s

The decade began with the separation of one of the sport's strongest ever driver line-ups as Prost left Senna at McLaren to join Ferrari. The pair continued to fight for supremacy both on and off the track, battling for wins while vying with each other to get the best seat at Williams, as their technologically advanced cars moved to the front. But everything was to change at Imola in 1994 in one of the most shocking weekends Formula One has ever seen.

Improvements in safety had made the sport complacent and the deaths of Senna and Roland Ratzenberger, who both perished at San Marino, instigated fundamental change.

Left: Benetton mechanic Paul Seaby is engulfed in flames during a disastrous Jos Verstappen pit stop at the 1994 German Grand Prix. Amazingly, Seaby survived the accident with only minor burns.

1990

After his controversial clash with Prost in Japan in 1989, Senna was facing a ban. He received a late reprieve and lined up with Berger at McLaren, with Prost now at Ferrari, but the end of the season proved that a leopard cannot change its spots. Senna started with victory in Phoenix, but Prost then took his first Ferrari win in Brazil, on Senna's home soil.

Prost won in Spain, and then came Japan. The pair lined up on row one, but when Senna started slowly he refused to concede the corner. They collided and Senna won the title. Piquet won the race for Benetton, as he did in Australia, but the Japan collision tarnished Senna's reputation.

1991

Reigning champion Senna was concerned by the pace of his new McLaren, but a great opening run put him in the driving seat early on. Senna took pole and victories in the first four races, but Piquet and Benetton broke the stranglehold in Canada.

Spa saw the debut of Michael Schumacher who, driving for the new Jordan team, qualified seventh but retired on lap one. Mansell hit back in Italy, where Schumacher scored his first points in fifth after moving to Benetton.
Senna won the title and handed victory in Japan to team-mate Berger before winning a shortened race in terrible conditions in Australia.

Above: Jean Alesi (Tyrrell 018 Ford) laps backmarker Michele Alboreto (Arrows A11B Ford) with Ayrton Senna (Mclaren MP4/5B Honda) hot on his heels behind at the 1990 United States Grand Prix.

1999

The decade closed as it began, with a clear battle between McLaren and Ferrari, but mid-season disaster for Schumacher left Irvine taking Ferrari's charge to the wire. Williams faltered and Jordan stepped up, with Frentzen joining Hill to become real contenders, while Villeneuve's promising new BAR team failed to deliver.

Schumacher's title challenge hit the skids in Britain when a leg-breaking crash put him out for six races. Coulthard won after pit mistakes by Häkkinen and Irvine, and when the McLaren pair collided at the start in Austria, Irvine took the win.

Frentzen won for Jordan in Italy, then Herbert took Stewart's first victory in a wet European Grand Prix. Schumacher returned for the new Malaysia race and fended off Häkkinen as Irvine led a Ferrari 1-2, but the Ulsterman failed at the final hurdle in Japan. Häkkinen took the title with a win as Irvine managed only third. Nevertheless, Ferrari was the constructors' champion as Formula One headed toward a new era.

Below: 1999 Malaysian Grand Prix: Eddie Irvine (Ferrari F399) closely followed by Mika Hakkinen (McLaren MP4/14 Mercedes). They finished in first and third positions respectively.

Michael Schumacher (Benetton B195 Renault) takes the checkered flag to win the 1995 French Grand Prix at Magny-Cours.

2006

Bidding for an eighth title, Schumacher matched Alonso at the head of the field, the pair filling the top two places in eight of 18 races as the old champion took the new one right down to the wire. The season saw the arrival of BMW, Honda, Toro Rosso, and Super Aguri while Jordan became Midland then Spyker.

Renault won the first three races, but Schumacher won in San Marino and Europe before Alonso embarked on a run of four. Ferrari and Schumacher fought back in the United States, then won again in France and Germany.

Schumacher closed the title gap with wins in Italy, where Alonso retired, and China, but retired in Japan and his long shot at the title went when Alonso won it with second in Brazil as Renault took the constructors' crown.

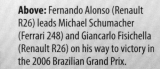

Above: Fernando Alonso (Renault R26) leads Michael Schumacher (Ferrari 248) and Giancarlo Fisichella (Renault R26) on his way to victory in the 2006 Brazilian Grand Prix.

2007

Alonso left Renault to create a turbulent partnership with team protegée Lewis Hamilton at McLaren, and Räikkönen filled Schumacher's big boots at Ferrari.

Räikkönen and Alonso started the season well and were dominant until Hamilton took his first victory in a stop-start crash-hit race in Canada. Hamilton won again in the United States before Räikkönen's season came back to life with wins in France and Britain. Räikkönen came back from 17 points behind and went on to win in Brazil and take the title by a point as Hamilton struggled to seventh.

2008

McLaren and Ferrari renewed their rivalry as Hamilton and Massa raced to another nail-bitingly tight title decider. Meanwhile, Alonso returned to Renault in a season that welcomed a new street circuit in Valencia and a night race in Singapore.

Kovalainen won in Hungary, but Massa dominated in Valencia and won again in the Belgian rain after Hamilton was disqualified for an illegal move in a battle with Räikkönen.

Italy saw a shock victory for Toro Rosso and Sebastian Vettel then Alonso won the night race in Singapore and the Japan Grand Prix where Massa and Hamilton collided. Massa won a thrilling race in Brazil and thought he had the title when Hamilton was sixth on the last lap, but the Briton made a last-gasp pass and stole the title by a point.

>>>>

Right: Jenson Button celebrates on the podium after winning the 2009 Spanish Grand Prix.

2009

The introduction of Kinetic Energy recovery System (KERS) and return of slick tyres made for an exciting season.

The season now stretched to 17 races starting in Australia and ending at the brand new circuit in Abu Dhabi. Ferrari and McLaren struggled to find form, and new constructor Brawn swept in. Button dominated the season, finally securing the title at the Brazilian Grand Prix. Brawn became the first constructor to win the constructors Championship in a debut season. Button became the 10th British driver to win the Championship.

2010

The 2010 season saw the introduction of a new track in Korea and drivers competing in 19 races overall.

Red Bull made an impressive comeback after failing to make their mark in the previous season. Red Bull went on to win the championship with their driver, Vettel, securing the driver's title after a tough battle with Button during the final race of the season at Abu Dhabi. Vettel became the youngest driver ever to win the championship. The 2010 season also saw world champion, Schumacher, come out of retirement.

2011

Vettell successfully defended his title in style winning the opening race after qualifying in pole position. He went on to emphatic wins in Malaysia, China, Turkey and Spain, but Button was close behind.

The championship came to a head in Japan where Vettel qualified just nine-thousandths of a second faster than Button for pole. Button went on to win the race, but Vettel made a podium finish, which was enough to secure the title for another year. During the last race of the season Vettel broke Mansell's record by securing his 15th pole position of the season.

Above: Hamilton takes the checkered flag to claim his maiden victory at the 2007 Canadian Grand Prix.

2012

2012 saw Vettell winning his third title for Red Bull by three points in the incident-packed Brazilian Grand Prix, making Vettell the youngest driver ever to win three world titles.

The huge 20-race season started as usual in Australia with a return to form from Alonso, but he was beaten by Button, who took an early lead from his team-mate, Hamilton. Alonso came back in Malaysia to steal the victory from Perez and Hamilton, who qualified in pole position once again. Vettel finished outside of the points and the championship looked wide open. Mercedes' controversial DRS design saw Nico Rosberg take pole and the victory for Mercedes and their first win as a constructor since 1955 in China. Despite political unrest and calls from human rights campaigners, including Amnesty International, for the race to be boycotted, the Bahrain Grand Prix went ahead and heralded a return to form from Vettel, who took the win and secured a lead at the top of the championship. Vettel capitalized on this victory by going on to win the championship.

Below: Jenson Button (Brawn BGP001 Mercedes) on his way to victory in the 2009 Spanish Grand Prix.

Index